Book of Bones

Kathy Gee

V.

Published in the United Kingdom in 2016
by V. Press,
10 Vernon Grove,
Droitwich,
Worcestershire,
WR9 9LQ.

ISBN: 978-0-9926114-4-6

Printed in the U.K. by Imprint Digital, Seychelles Farm, Upton Pyne,
Exeter EX5 5HY, on recycled paper stock.

V.

Contents

V.

V.

"Every contact leaves a trace"
(Edmond Locard, 1877-1966)

V.

V.

Grave goods

Take me in my shed to Berrow Hill,
arrange me in a deckchair,
treasures hung from roof to floor:
a barbecue, guitar and secateurs,
with olive oil to ease my passing,
curry in six stoneware pots,
a case of Macon in the corner,
tea pot, after-dinner mints.
Stuff every gap with history books
and, when the shed is full, pile up
a mound of English earth.
Place oak-wood benches on the top
to give a view along the river.

Visit me on Mondays, hear my echo,
write to me from time to time.

Woman to woman

(Cueva de la Pileta, Spain)

Like every daughter and their sisters,
we must climb the mountain
where the ancestors have led the way.
Our Elder Mother takes us to the entrance,
hands us powdered ash and ochre.

Stepping into dark, I wait till spirits
lead me forward, brighten black
with suns that only we may carry. Light
in dark, we leave our signs – outside
within – my charcoal, praising hand.

Our voices echo round the chamber,
touching rock where all is born.
We leave our gifts of water,
shoals of fish in red and black and ochre,
plenty for our children's children.

Linking hands with Earth, our breathing
makes us one. Like daughters gone before,
we summon all the spirits of the sea.

Goats infuse the air of Spanish day,
their bleats confused with welcome.

Carla climbs to join us, oils the lock.

She lights the hurricane to flare and spit
like ancient brushwood torches,

lifts her lamp to darkness, showing

hands. More hands. Their fingers
spread in charcoaled outline. Greeting

palm to palm, they guard the future,

shoals of fish in red and black and ochre
drawn where only children reach.

We're almost touching hands
in darkness, half way up a mountain,
thirty thousand years apart.

Advice to the ancestors

Decide before the gods step in,
before the breath that takes you down.

Do not associate with gold
or anything that raises lust.
Don't go to ground with comb or sword:
no gifts will speed your onward passage.

It could happen – treasures lifted,
long bones brushed and tickled, rows
of loose jaws laughing at the sky
or, worse, the inside of a show case.

Sign up to oblivion,
take my advice and choose cremation.

Book of bones

Your flesh has gone, left only bone,
anonymous as x-rays. Notches
in the pelvis tell of sex
without the curves of fatty comfort
you had moulded over time.

You could be (plus or minus) dated
by disintegrating carbon.
DNA shows ancestry,
and tooth enamel proves that you
were Yorkshire, faking southern ways.

We find no trace of intellect;
ideas cannot linger in the bone.

Convert in Cathedral Close

I've got to know you bone by bone.
I know the lie you hoped would die,
laid bare your secret, final deal.

Beneath my trowel, your Saxon toes
should spread like ivory on clay.
Instead they lie like tumbled dice
in dirty white on a charcoal bed.
Your feet point east as Christians' do
but pagan rites were what you trusted:
songs of passage, sacred ashes
hot beneath your doubting body.

Digging done, this caring church
will box your bones to meet their God.
There's no escaping heaven now.

A whiff of scandal

A khaki smell approaches sideways,
leaks round bins, past tangled fern
and mud to prick the city's nostrils.

Reptile writers lick-flick sources –
this is not an honest cloudburst
flooding overheated gutters.

No, what draws attention is a smear
of roast, sour grapes and lumpy gravy.
Sleaze or dirt, a trace of sick,

the crust of last night's guacamole.
This is where they rest, the dregs.
A glob of fat that blocks the drain.

Stalker

Lights switch themselves on
in corridors that are his
until dawn.

He collects dead papers,
precisely straightens chairs
to prospectus perfection.

Using latex gloves
he clears the debris
round the tea urn,

searches for the lipstick pout
on a cup he knows
she leaves for him.

His lips seek hers,
the tip of his tongue
positioning itself on the rim,

flooding his mouth with liquid.

Second skin

Madam, this is recommended:
Sherwood's Adjustable Bustle and Skirt.
Eliminates compression
from the female spine and heart.
Or Thomson's Patent Glove Fit Corset,
First For Comfort, almost undetectable,
gives graceful contour to the form
with added snaps and latch for safety.

Virtuous young women welcome
busk, suspenders, whalebone, lacing.
For the sake of reputation,
Madam, this is recommended.

Prince Edward's banished lover

Florence Trevelyan, d. 1907, Sicily.

She left him for the money,
her ample pay-off compensating
for a reputation left behind.
Occasionally she would meet
a courtier in the *passegiata,*
see a faint smile leave their lips
before a very British snub.

She told the locals half the truth
and built a cliff-side English garden.
Terracotta terraces
cast fish-scale shadows on the path
as lizards quietly accepted her,
exploring upside down on the bark
of her newly planted cypress trees.

She loved the beat of their tiny lungs,
their brave defiance of gravity.

Stripped

A long six months since the front door slammed
on his parting shot, she starts to look for colour,
peels back rotten layers, finds bare wood.

There's high-gloss black, re-coated every decade
by the sweet shop lady's father's father,
then red oxide, 'borrowed' by a tenant
who maintained the village needle mill.

And under that, the blue of sugar bags,
the paint demanded by a new-wed wife
to cover tallow-spatters round the hearth.

Beneath the blue is optimistic lime-wash:
stops the rot and still the best for damp.
It ends with naked oak, a forest tree
that died the day that Henry killed Queen Anne.

They say

(OS Grid Ref: SP 22536 65012)

In the second winter of the plague, forked lightning
struck an oak that stood alone above the valley,
left its trident bones to guard the unploughed fields.

They say that daughters of the land returned to dance
among the elder bushes, crones reclaiming earth.

One night a traveller in hood and garter found
the place at dusk as vents of smoke arose from nowhere,
found a dozen cats who drummed with mandrake roots.

They say the feline sisters fed him cloves and wine,
drew circles round his feet and sang him to the flames.

Act V, scene 4

My father should be proud,
the most impressive house in town.
Close-studded timbers, herringbone,
an orchard, bee boles, herbs,
the purple stain of mulberries.

No alderman ignores me
living proud on High Street,
far from pedlars, butcher's boys
and maids abroad in Swine Street.
That is where I find my money,

in the crowd of bawds and ostlers,
passing lords and their attendants.
Characters can be transformed
to enemies and friends. I give
them words, they give me wealth.

One day these streets will fill
with scripted patter, tour guides,
foreign currency and tips.
My merchandise is language,
coining all the words I need
for deeds beyond imagination.

Traces

There must be blood in a house this old.
A scalp wound from the water wheel,
forefinger lost to beet-hook on an icy day,
a knife distracted at the kitchen range.

No trace of death remains
though someone must have died,
perhaps unnoticed, sleeping by the fire,
or a fatal stroke in the upstairs room,
where weight and winding stairs
required that coffin-hole cut through
the floorboards. Still convenient, in case.

No sign recalls the distant killing
brought to her front door by men in hats.
There's something in their downcast eyes,
their forward movement, circled arms,
anticipates her slow collapse. Her floury
fingerprints slide whispers down the frame.

Called

They called and so I went,
climbed up the slope and said
goodbye to the fallow deer,
their ears transparent in the sun.
Walked up, and on, away.

Father left my *Farmers Weekly*
and my rabbit gun untouched.
But they would read my name
on the way to church
and think of me at Christmas.
Annie's children too, they knew.

Three words, the letters carved
by someone who came back,
who cried in the mason's yard
for *Private Thomas Luxton.*
More than just another name.

Timing

You could have walked the moorland road
to a long horizon, stayed an extra hour with friends
and talked of otters at their hazel plot.

You could have chosen to use the motorway,
stopped for coffee, bought a bar of chocolate,
spent some minutes parked beneath a tree.

If you'd done any of those things, the fox
would still have darted through the hawthorn hedge
in search of pigeons on the other side.

But then it would be someone else
jack-hammered into a Ford Fiesta,
toffee papers blowing in the wind.

Ghost bike

He leaves the zebra crossing
on his birthday mountain bike
steers white rubber treads through crowds

Standing on white pedals
he powers whitened handlebars
past women buying flowers wrapped in cellophane
past grief as brief as poppies
mounts the pavement, races

back past shrines of plastic bag
bouquets tied high on lamp posts
back down Nelson Road and Churchill Avenue
past scented rosemary to where
the grannies lead him home

His small white-painted bike is chained to railings
padlock shaking every time
a lorry turns

Ghost bikes are painted white and locked to street furniture
near to where the cyclist was killed.

News from now

Dear Frank and William Styler,
Wilfred Slade and Arthur Watton,

Not much changes
you'll be pleased to know,
though recently we cut the nettles
for another row of graves.
All your folk have moved away,
your stories gone. The stone says
        Edgar Badger, Cecil Burrow,
        Egbert Dolphin, brother John.

I wish that you could hear the bees,
the sound of batsmen at the nets.
Jackdaws wearing balaclavas
strut the belfry; yew trees creak
and scare young children in the night.
The fields of buttercups and vetch
are bright as when you died.
We're going to sow red poppies
in the playground,
        Alfred Gould and Ernest Pearce,
        Alick Pretty, Harry Richmond

        We are,
            most respectfully,
                yours.

Déjà vu

Black Country Living Museum

He finds a photograph of Aunty Cissie
in the guide book, blouse as crisp
as when he clung with bitten nails
to wait for Ma, for bread and bacon tea.

He hears her echo down the alley,
past the lock where Albert drowned a cat,
the ring of hobnail boots on Chapel kerb.
By the time he finds the privy in the yard,
he's living twice but slightly out of synch.

He chats with volunteers in pinafores,
remembers entries, passages, front-parlours,
strokes the leaded range and wonders
how they know so much about his life.

Death's Head Ward

We're specimens on metal trollies,
only lighting up when someone comes
to slow the natural process of decay.

Our cabinets are meant to be dust free
but mites get in, create their tumbleweed
and breed in sterile crevices.

Those in charge assume that nothing
happens in their absence, taxonomies
lie still between the paper sheets.

We prefer to leave in darkness,
flutter through each last remaining breath
to seek the light of somewhere new.

Provenance

Somewhere in the swirl of paint
lies moisture captured from his breath,
some slight impression of his gaze,
the weight of hours in a draughty loft.

Collectors breathe the painter's dust,
observe as women stitch their silks
and sunlight falls on a chequered floor.
They want to own the artist's essence,
touching atoms, brushing fingers,
seeking to be part of him,
his fame illuminating theirs.

Goering, finding his Vermeer
was fake, was shocked, as if he'd just
discovered there is evil in the world.

Reversal

In the Cellar Mirror, Norman Blamey.
Government Art Collection.

They are portraits in a mirror,
posed with foreign postcards wedged
between the glass and wooden frame.

Their eyes are distanced by reflection,
pensive, waiting for our crowd
to move aside and clear their view.

Today they see a gallery,
tomorrow maybe politicians,
children or an empty room.

They stare beyond the frame at us,
exchanging thoughts of might have been.

Taking a likeness

The Old Pilot, 1884, watercolour, William Wainwright.
Penlee House Gallery and Museum, Penzance.

I wonder if those folds of clothing ever
peel apart? I'm sure he sleeps in knitted
rib – adrift in baccy, brine and herring ...

> *Don't feel right just sat here, lazy,*
> *stuck inside to face his easel.*
> *Went down to the slip and waited,*
> *ready to be picked for sixpence.*
> *Dirty weather. Easy money.*

... must be sixty, knows the Newlyn harbour
like his trouser pocket. Draw his outline,
right eye large from years of telescope ...

> *It's hot in all this clobber. Florence*
> *says a man should never wear*
> *his hat indoors. I tell him tales*
> *of peril, true they are and tragic,*
> *likely worth an extra tuppence.*

... the wash behind must swirl like rippled sand,
translucent, brown as flooding tides in winter.
Let the paper show through fraying serge ...

> *Circling seagulls up already,*
> *always first to know, those birds.*
> *I wait to hear our fishwives calling,*
> *fear the sound of crashing waves,*

a wailing from the harbour wall.

... add detail, finest brush, dark blue and ochre.
Think I'll call it "In the Face of Danger".
Memories and loss sell well.

Earthquake in Stoke-on-Trent

Slip and bone are on the move
as Gaia shrugs her shoulders.

Every gorgeous, gilded piece
starts walking in a china army.
Minton, Spode and Copeland
chitter – cartoon figures taking
tiny rocking steps across the glass.
Vibration clatters saucers, teapots,
tin glaze, soft paste, Wedgwood blue.

Transfixed curators watch the distance
to the front edge of the shelf.

Unacceptable

Stretched on her stomach, she gropes
in the dark for relics gathered
at the time that Darwin climbed
this marble staircase – caused a riot
with his Evolution lecture.

No electric light to pierce
the boarded gloom, she works by touch,
pulls re-used boxes into daylight.
Army and Navy, Home and Colonial,
Oxo tins, suspicious bundles.

Shadows spew out souvenirs.
Bronze coinage from the Opium Wars,
a mirror from the Cawnpore well.
Her blackened fingers pick up echoes,
share her dust with distant Empire.

In the furthest, darkest corner:
dry, unravelled rope. A leather
tennis ball that blinks in the dark.
The shrunken head she almost drops
will not be shown to modern eyes.

Found in the freezer

The emperor penguin
never spent a winter
huddled with an egg
at minus sixty,
died in a Yorkshire zoo.

He rests in his plastic bag
between a loggerhead
turtle and two civet cats.
A feathered torpedo
lulled by mechanical hum,

awaiting his turn to stand
on a fibreglass iceberg,
poised to dive
through painted waters.

Orientation

A map is not the landscape,
shows the journey, not its ending,
knows the road but cannot tell you
how to find your way.

Life's a chart of known unknowns
where here-be-dragons curl
and monsters guard the Empty Quarter.

This is nothing new. Don't worry.
Home is always split
between at least three different maps.
We live beyond the contour lines.

Northerner in the South

He's still a stranger in a country
where he knows he's been adopted,

has that uncooked look, as if
he used to understand much more.

Thin skin put on each morning, helps
to hold his bones together. Dis-

located, out of class, he lives
in spaces smaller than his mind.

He'll never lose the absence, always
hold its grit within his oyster.

Stratified

Her Yorkshire vowels are horizontal, flat
as glacial lakes, as hard as millstone grit.

A flirt with narrow Midland intonation
overlaid her voice with potter's clay,
with carved and bevelled valleys, furrows
curved by oxen, cut by railway lines.

Then Devon granite, schist and mudstone
mimicked in the burr of rolling hills,
the verbal turn of tors in rain and heather,
all the gravelled wash of stormy seas.

This voice is earthed in layered bedrock,
burnished by her metamorphic years.

I am George Washington's axe

Perhaps I didn't trek the Himalayas,
never snorkelled from a small canoe
off the coast of Zanzibar. Perhaps
that woman met with generals, not I.

My hair, my eyelashes, my skin
have been refreshed each seven years
and so there should be nothing left
to recognise at the school reunion.

Philosophers conclude that if its shape
and purpose stay the same, then
with its two new heads and three new hafts,
it's still George Washington's axe.

If I met her, the one I knew aged ten,
I don't know what we'd talk about.
And yet I have fulfilled her dreams,
hold all her memories on ice.

I saw that woman in the mirror
on her wedding day and knew
that she was beautiful.

Examined

The Corn Laws, never needed now,
recall the rub of scuffling elbows,
rust-red carpets laid out on the lawn,
all musty from the cycle shed.
Then Glaciation, with the scent
of orange blossom, raspberries,
of dew-damp earth, of apple shade
and Cox's Orange Pippin.
Finally, the rhythmic roll of syllables,
the tongue and ear of Bovary,
of Moliere, whose yellow *pensées*
laughed beside the lemonade.
Revision wasn't wasted then,
suffused with hormones, seventeen.

Backpack

When I leave, I'll take a map
with elsewhere on the folded edge.

I'll fill my veins with hedgerow gin,
my mind with friendly voices, hands
with cake and green tomatoes
stolen from my lover's garden.

Keys I'll never use again
will jangle through the warmth
of sleeping terriers, release
the locks that make me stay.

Don't start to worry. Vultures
don't yet soar like vengeance
over burning wagons. This
is only planning. If I leave,

I'll wear my rucksack to the front,
to stop me looking back.

Exchange rate

Say another hundred Cairo pounds.
Another eighty then, it's nothing to you,
you who walked into my shop,
who drank my apple tea, and who I know
appreciates this beauty, longs to own
the flower-scattered meadow of my quilt.
You love the square of butterflies
I know, but it's too much. Look, this
you can afford. You see the letters,
arabesque and interlace, the colours
and sweet symmetry of land and Nile.
The maker doesn't use a pattern,
cuts by eye and will not bargain.
Not like you, my lady, who will give me
just another fifty pounds. Oh, lady,
if it must be so, then let's shake hands,
agree a thousand. And two kisses.

Picturing Ta Prohm

My dark is thick with frog song,
leather leaves slow falling, echoing
the bok bok chorus.

Wait. Allow your skin to breathe
the wrap of humid air, your ears to hear
my tendril roots caressing stone.

Stand still. Watch dawn light up
my canopy, transform my shade
to velvet drapes of moss and lichen.

Stay your shutter finger. Listen.
Feel the weight of my decay.

Shots

He shoots her,
posed in cream for contrast,
by the staircase urn
of scarlet lilies.

She shoots him,
staring into the lens,
beige with oleander flowers,
slouched before a mountain.

He shoots a dozen
distant views of steam trains
framed by palm trees.
One of the cathedral.

She shoots him,
chin on hand,
elbow on his knee
with one foot on the balcony.

Usually it's her
that tries to capture him,
to keep him with her,
just in case.

Moon-gazing hare

You've watched him wait
for a change of heart, for her
to shine again for him.

His time is carved in ivory.
Each lift of breath draws dreams
he can't resist. They fill his night.

At dawn he sighs alone
through fields of ox-eye daisies,
longing for the migrant's song.

He hoards his scrap of hope
among the nettles. You use yours
to wrap his heart in dock leaves.

Seek out woundwort for yourself.
Your waiting mustn't wait on his.

The moment

Was it when we turned at Strete,
where once your granddad's Rover
crashed the only other car in town,

or at the cottage where we danced
in lines between the rafters, ceiling
hung so low that tall men had to stoop,

or when we walked with dogs
and seagulls through the rain
and fought the wind that forced us back?

I only knew that it was love
when evening tied a band
of silk brocade across my chest

and knowing you existed
warmed my skin with wishes
even though we were apart.

Summer house

I walk these paths in search of ghosts,
my morning footsteps hesitant
and wet from last night's rain.

Our secret hut is still unlocked,
blue painted planks fade in the sun.
I gently push the door

to find us gone. Some other's tears
have stained the empty envelope,
bleached dry upon the floor.

Death to the inner destroyer

I'm going to kill my archivist.
I hate him when he talks between
my thumbs on the steering wheel.
I hate how he uses my name in full:
Oh, Kathryn, no. For heaven's sake.
He makes me agonise aloud, recall
events long gone I can't put right.

My archivist should concentrate
on cataloguing happy moments.
Not a chance. He sniffs around the dirt
on my shoes like a rat in the darkness.
Scruffy and rancid, he pushes his neuron
trolley of fog, brings up grey plastic trays
of regret from storage deep in the stack.

He snivels in his cork-soled shoes,
appears in the silence, testing my mettle
with the squeak of his wheels. He finds
me out, pursues me down the corridor
with bundles tied in document tape.
He perseveres.
He perseveres.

I'm going to burn his acid-free boxes,
turn off the air-con, take back his key.

Thanks a bunch, Ted Hughes

It was your poems on the college wall
that made me think *memento mori*.

Perhaps some memory of me will last,
at least while friends are still alive,
and my research, my small additions
to a narrow field, will surface in a library.

My poems might be found in stapled leaflets,
Oxfam's lowest shelf; a hardback afterlife
of sorts in the shiny coffee-table book:
my closing poem in Great British Gardens.

Someone's going to find it second hand
and wonder who the hell this woman was.

1950s' teak wardrobe, £50 o.n.o

There should be jackets, shirts
and suits, a stripy dressing gown.
And ties – a man's life history
in flashes of heraldic colour, coiled
like snakes in glass compartments.

Or there might be endless winter,
trees where time stands still.
There might be packs of wolves,
or goblins hiding in a raincoat, frogs
that lurk in polished brogues.

And there could be my father,
turning round to stretch his hand,
to pull me up to join him.

Parenting

I prepare a coffee thermos, hoping he won't know
it's Jameson's not Scotch, then slice roast beef,
although it's never thin enough,
and search the wardrobe for a rucksack
he will try to carry, for a while.
I wait for him, arriving late with his plastic bag:
his soft white bread, a jar of sugar, English mustard.

We have to go through rituals, refuse
to turn the starter key until he's belted up,
then he will side-seat drive me to distraction
eight long miles to park at Cantor Hill.

He stumbles at the stile where mud is churned,
a trembling in his knees, the grey
around his mouth held tight in deeper lines.
I take the rucksack till we reach the car.
He leans on the bonnet, checks in the mirror,
draws a comb through his wilting quiff, says
Who will take you walking when I'm eighty?

Seeing is believing

He last saw Mum in the hospice,
where she said her last goodbye:
Well, have it your own way, dear.
He took her favourite earrings, cream
enamel, dark red lily in the centre,
asked the nurse to clip them on
and she looked ... beautiful.
She'd gone on his last visit, lips
and skin sunk from her teeth,
her weighted earlobes bent by dying.
So he told them, you can take her.

Years before, he drove a day
to view his Dad. The undertaker's
lad 'prepared' him – quilted satin,
powder, curly hair combed flat.
He couldn't leave. He roared
and stamped until he found a step
where cool breath touched him,
let him find the door and go.

But that was better than the first time.
Dave died in the water, lost for weeks,
in no fit state for viewing. Even now,
he finds it hard to believe.

The unforgotten twin

In the bay window, a wheelchair
turns its back on beds to give
a birthday moment of normality.

How old are you, Olive? says Nurse.
I'm sixty eight the wheelchair says.
Oh bless her, she means eighty six.

And how many children, Olive?
Three adults at her knee await
the answer... give it for her:

three they smile in unison.
Their mother firmly contradicts
No, four... I had four.

Memory fish

Gather up those pondweed corpses.
Let them dry upon a stone.

Surprise yourself when strength
returns like bone through drying skin.
The body first – the head takes time.

One day in spring, come home
to find the shoal has swum away.
Except the one that hurts you most.

Cling on despite yourself,
preserve it for a month, a year,
surprised that it can take so long.

When time alone is not enough,
throw the blighted thing away.

The Unbeliever

(For Barbara, ordained 2013)

Arriving late, I catch a glimpse
in the chapter house.
A white gowned figure
standing, votive, with her circle.

The organ sounds a fanfare.
I'd like to sing the unfamiliar tune
but I am outside looking in.
The grace notes dart like swallows
through the stone arcade:
Do nothing from ambition or conceit.
Look only to the good of others,
rooted and grounded in love.
Well, yes. All that is fine.

Another life is offered up.
The Bishop places slender hands
upon her temples, presses
the promise deep to her bones.
Will you support and encourage her?
Yes, of course I will.
I don't believe in God
but I do believe in Barbara.

The cross and book procession
draws her to the light,
to the rarely open Great West Door
which closes firmly at her back.

B Minor Mass

A flock of scores
stand curving into light
like seagull wings.

The countertenor's
sharp crescendos cut
the blur of wood pigeons.

Sopranos swoop
in murmuration, swirling
clouds of semibreves.

The baritone spreads eagle wings
with pinions fanned to ride the thermal.
Waves of sound repeat and surge,
weave under, up and back, ascending.
All the birds of field and forest pause.

A fluting curlew brings
pale hope beyond the storm.
In Agnus Dei, peace.

A woman's body

Cut me through to count the rings,
my circled cells of aging, fed
and watered in fat times and thin.

In storms, this heart-wood kept me
rooted, standing firm when forest fires
dropped flecks of carbon on my skin.

Whoever cares to look will find
eruptions blocked the sun,
yet spring draws sap to happy leaves.

Don't grieve my felling. Cut me through
and you'll find climate, not just weather.
Mostly it's been temperate.

Six hours at Llanrhidian

Thrift shakes papery heads in the wind
as sheep process like stilted dowagers
across the marsh to the turning tide.

A dinner-suited wagtail spirals up
to block the path of a ewe on a mission,
leading lambs through samphire, herb and rush

where waves of ripples swallow shallows,
tickle the upturned hull of a cockle boat.
Small islands faint beneath the water,

meet the moment. River, sea and marsh
are one. A grey-cloaked heron lifts his baton,
sending time slow-sucking back again.

V.

V.

Acknowledgements

'Provenance' uses a much quoted final phrase, said to be from "Goering's biographer", original source unknown. The corsets in 'Second skin' came from American mail order catalogues. The names in 'News from now' are on the Feckenham war memorial. The ethnographic collections described in 'Unacceptable' are held by the Torquay Natural History Society. 'The Unbeliever' quotes the Church of England service for the ordination of deacons.

Thanks are due to those editors who published earlier versions of these poems: Stalker and Ghost bike – *Obsessed by Pipework*, Taking a likeness – *Angle*, Examined – *Antiphon*, Picturing Ta Prohm – *And Other Poems*, Second skin and The unforgotten twin – *Ink, Sweat and Tears*, The Unbeliever – *Acumen.*

I should also like to thank Stephen Boyce and Alison Brackenbury who encouraged me to take my poetry seriously; the Worcestershire Stanza group, especially Sarah James, John Lawrence and Jenna Plewes; the Edge poets – Rosie Miles, Nicola Slee and Penny Hewlett; and friends Sylvia Hunter, Lew Bennett, Barbara Wheatley and Sue Wilkinson. Jo Bell's excellent '52' prompts stimulated some of these pieces – her mentoring and criticism, along with the friendship and creative friction of members of 52, are legendary.

Finally, huge thanks to Sarah James and Ruth Stacey at V. Press, whose wisdom, skill and patience are boundless.

V.

V.